INTRODUCTION

IN THE MIDDLE AGES, before the full development of modern firearms, soldiers fought with swords, bows-and-arrows, battle-axes and other similar weapons. Special high-ranking soldiers called knights fought for their king or other lord to whom they owed their loyalty. In battle (or in the contests called jousts) they rode on horseback, fought with swords and lances (in a joust the object was simply to use the lance to unseat the mounted opponent), and, for protection, wore metal armor and carried shields.

From the pieces in this book you can construct a paper replica of an English knight as he would have appeared around the year 1416, just after the battle of Agincourt, in which the English fought the French on French soil. This was an episode of the Hundred Years' War (1337–1453), a long-drawn-out struggle between England and France for possession of certain territories in what since then has remained part of France.

The armor worn by our knight consists of a combination of metal plate and chain mail (interlinked metal rings). Over a chain-mail skirt and metal-plate-covered torso, he wears a cloth *jupon*, bearing the heraldic devices of King Henry V of England, well known to audiences and readers of Shakespeare's plays. The small helmet he wears is called a *bascinet*, over which the *great helm*, or larger helmet, is placed. The lance he carries is used to attempt to unseat an opponent on horseback. The sword in his scabbard (an extra, unsheathed, sword is also provided here) is for use in closer combat or when fighting unmounted.

The tools you will need to make the knight are (1) scissors; (2) a hobby knife, such as an X-ACTO knife with a #11 blade; (3) white glue, such as Elmer's or Sobo; (4) a tool for scoring, such as a dull paring knife or butter knife; (5) a ruler or other firm straight-edged object; and (6) a tool, such as a spoon or popsicle stick, that you can use to press the pieces firmly together when they have been glued.

Before beginning to put together the pieces, study the cover photograph and the diagrams to see how the pieces are supposed to fit together. Also read through the instructions before cutting out anything. Now examine the individual parts. You will notice that many pieces have tabs that are to be folded and glued to other pieces (each of these tabs has a dot on it). Your work will be neater if you score the lines along the tabs before you make the fold. Do this by tracing along the lines with a scoring tool (as mentioned above), using a ruler or other straightedge as a guide. Press hard enough to make a slight groove in the paper, but not so hard that you cut through it. (Some tabs, like those on the shaft of the lance, work better when reverse-scored, that is, scored on the *underside* of the paper.)

Carefully cut out the pieces one at a time, as you need them. Before gluing any pieces together, be sure that they are the correct ones and that they fit. When you are satisfied that the pieces are in their proper places, carefully glue them together. When applying glue to a tab, apply it *only* to the tab, not the receiving surface. Do not use too much glue—it will seep out and cause a mess. Keep a damp tissue or sponge handy so that you can quickly wipe glue away if you get any where you don't want it. For neater results, use a spoon or similar tool to press down on and smooth out the parts that you have just glued. Make sure the glue is dry before you handle glued pieces.

Now you may begin assembling the knight. Start by scoring, cutting out and gluing together the front and rear pieces for the mail skirt. Before you glue them together, glue the tabs of each separate piece in place. To give these pieces curvature it is helpful to pull the inside over the edge of a table before gluing the tabs in place. This may also be done with any of the other pieces for the knight that are curved in any way. Next, cut out and form the breast- and backplate, and then glue it to the mail skirt. Reverse-score the tabs on the body insert and glue this piece inside the mail skirt, with the tabs, pointing downward, just out of sight along the edge.

Now set aside the torso you have just formed, and assemble the legs and leg armor. Begin with the left and right greaves (or you may assemble all the parts of one leg at a time). Be sure to glue the leg inserts in place (similar to the gluing in of the body insert) before gluing the cuisses to the greaves, the next step. Form and glue together the soles and sollerets next, and carefully place the straps and spurs over the sollerets, gluing together the two sides of each spur around the back of each solleret. Glue the greaves to the inside of the assembled foot pieces. Be sure all the parts of the legs are lined up, as shown in the diagrams. When you are satisfied with the alignment of the legs, assemble the knee cops and glue them in place around the knees.

Next assemble the arms, starting with the rerebraces and vambraces. Glue the cuffs around the vambraces (with the seams facing in toward where the body will be) before gluing in the gauntlets. To give proper shape to the hands, score along the knuckles of the gauntlets; also score and fold in the inside strip of the index fingers (next to the thumbs), gluing the little tabs in place to hold the shape. The elbow cops are similar in form and function to the knee cops; each, however, is formed of only one piece. Glue these in place, and then set aside the arms.

Next assemble the bascinet (showing the knight's face). The body is formed of one piece and the cap of two pieces glued together. Glue the assembled cap to the top of the body piece, and then set aside the bascinet. If you do not plan to glue the great helm in place permanently, cut out and form the coronet and glue it just under the top edge of the body of the bascinet, over the knight's eyes. (With the great helm glued in place, the coronet cannot be seen and is therefore not necessary.)

The great helm is assembled in a manner similar to that of the bascinet. Notice that it has a body formed of *two* pieces, as well as a bottom rim that is glued in place after the cap and body have been assembled.

You are now ready to join the major pieces to form the knight. You will need to add a few other pieces. You may cut out and have ready the motons and gorget now, if you wish, but it is best to leave the pauldrons on the page until you need them.

Glue the legs to the body insert in the torso, where marked. Make adjustments if necessary to give the knight's stance a natural look. The feet should be pointed slightly outward. Cut out the belts. Glue the wide belt to circle the hips, and the narrow belt so it hangs diagonally over the wide belt. Cut out the two halves of the sword-and-scabbard, glue them together and glue this piece to the narrow belt so that the scabbard hangs under the left arm.

(Text continues after Plates.)

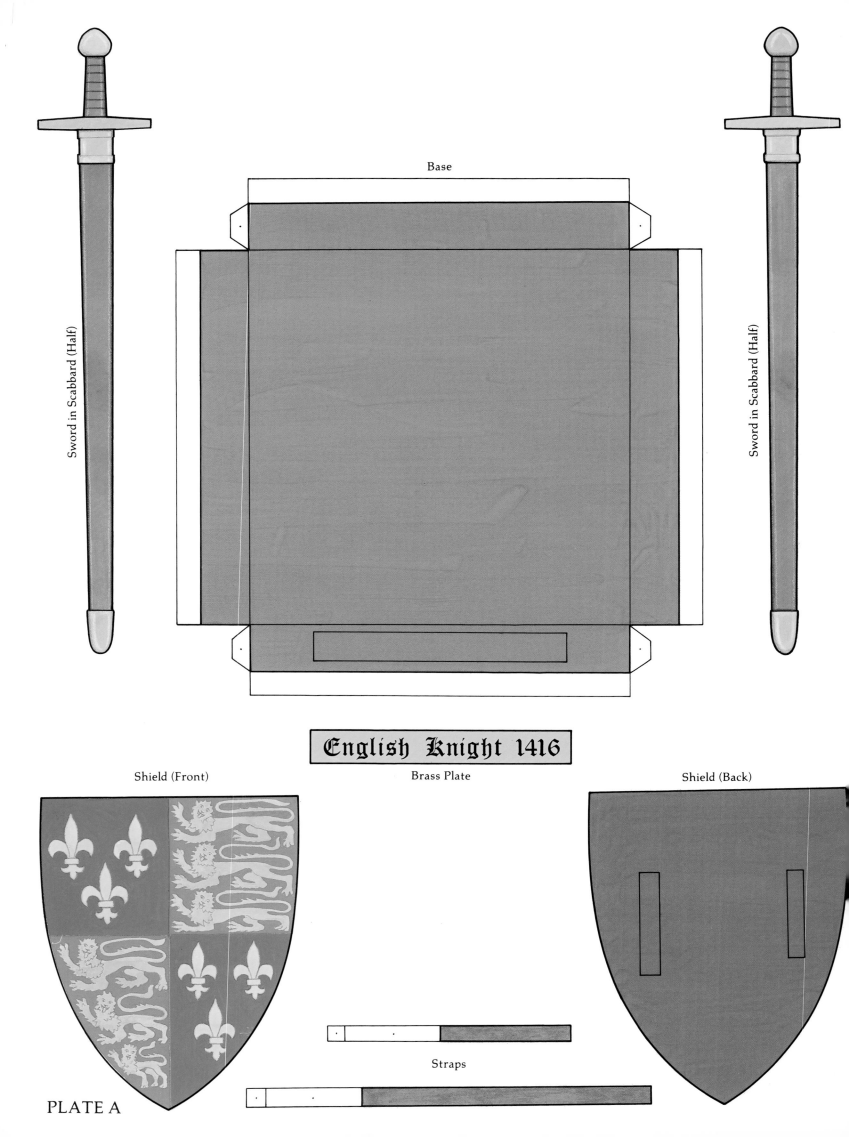

Base

Sword in Scabbard (Half)

Sword in Scabbard (Half)

English Knight 1416

Shield (Front)

Brass Plate

Shield (Back)

Straps

PLATE A

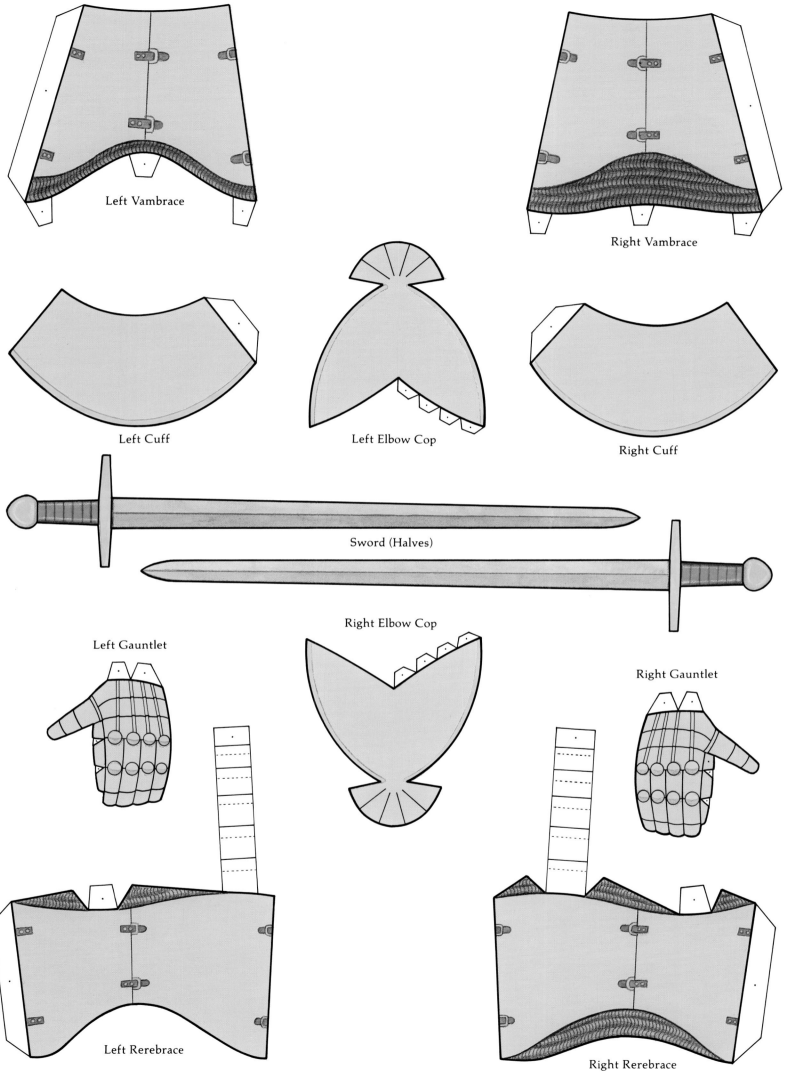

Left Vambrace

Right Vambrace

Left Cuff

Left Elbow Cop

Right Cuff

Sword (Halves)

Left Gauntlet

Right Elbow Cop

Right Gauntlet

Left Rerebrace

Right Rerebrace

PLATE B

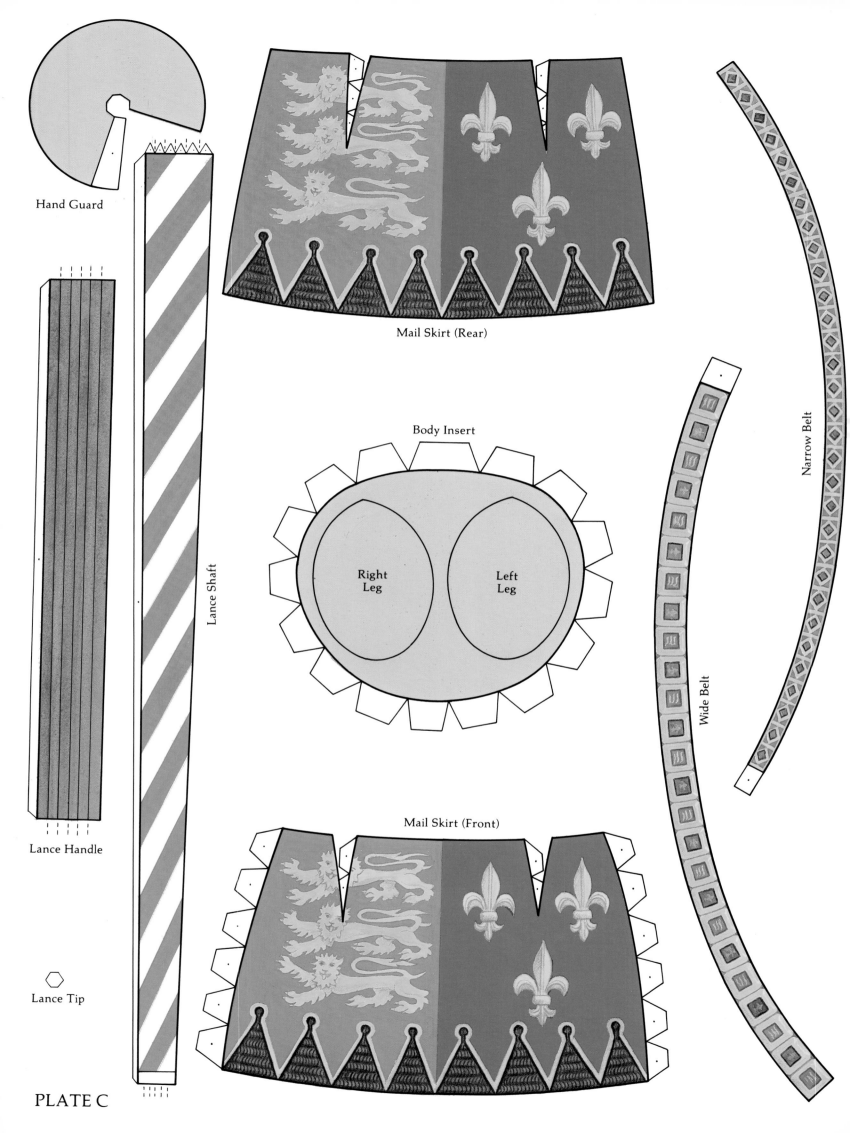

Hand Guard

Mail Skirt (Rear)

Narrow Belt

Lance Shaft

Body Insert

Right Leg

Left Leg

Wide Belt

Lance Handle

Lance Tip

Mail Skirt (Front)

PLATE C

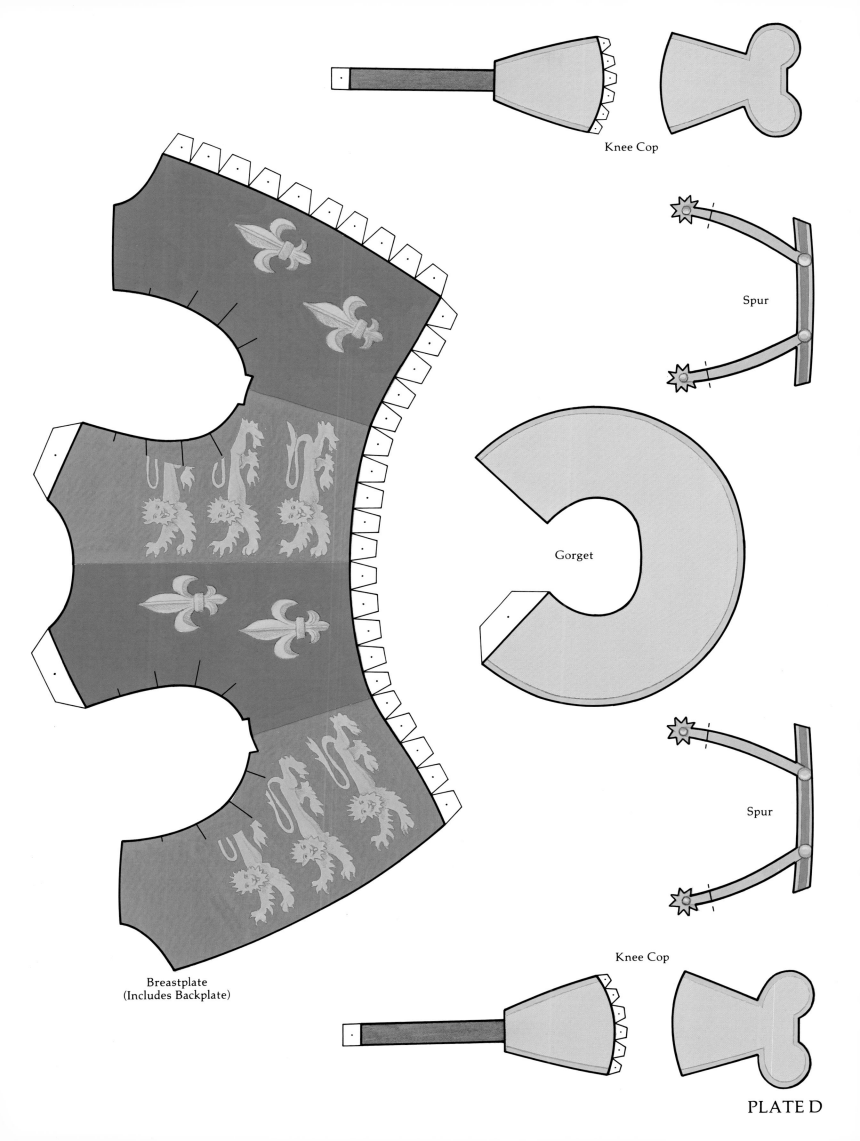

Knee Cop

Spur

Gorget

Spur

Knee Cop

Breastplate
(Includes Backplate)

PLATE D

I

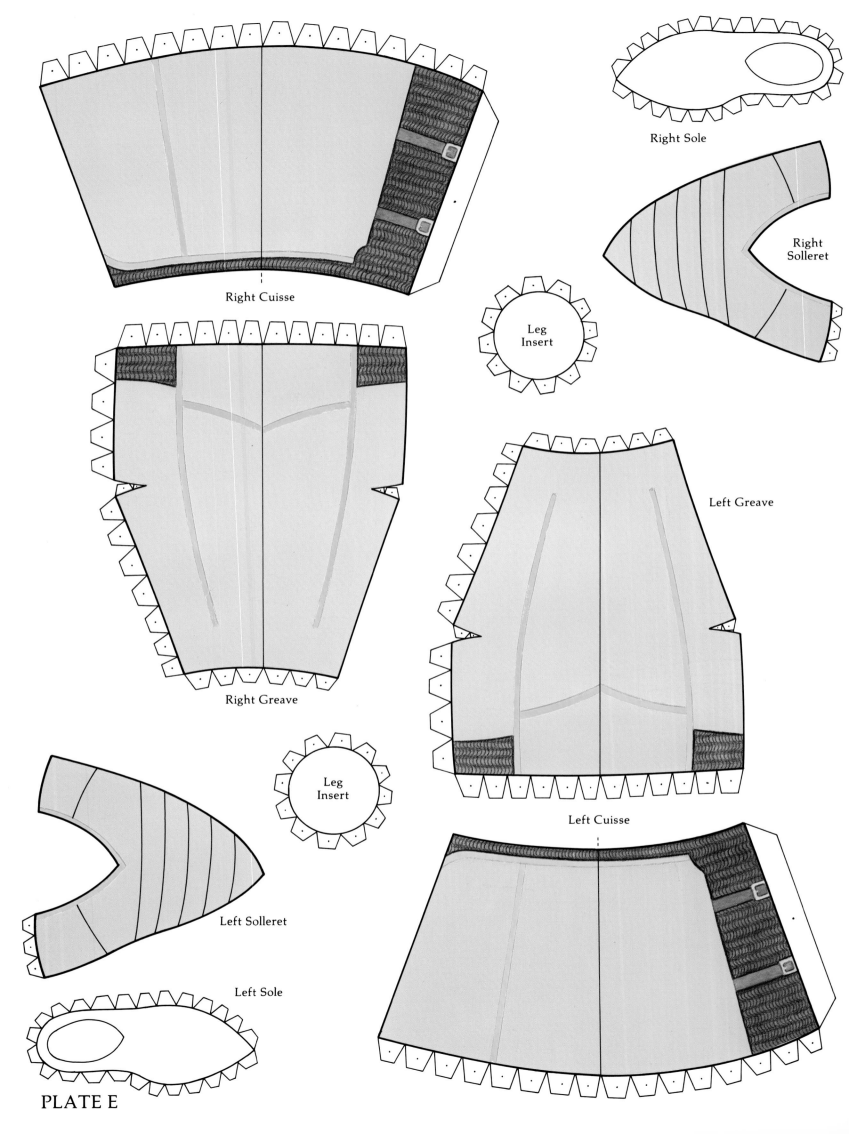

Right Cuisse

Right Sole

Right
Solleret

Leg
Insert

Right Greave

Left Greave

Leg
Insert

Left Cuisse

Left Solleret

Left Sole

PLATE E

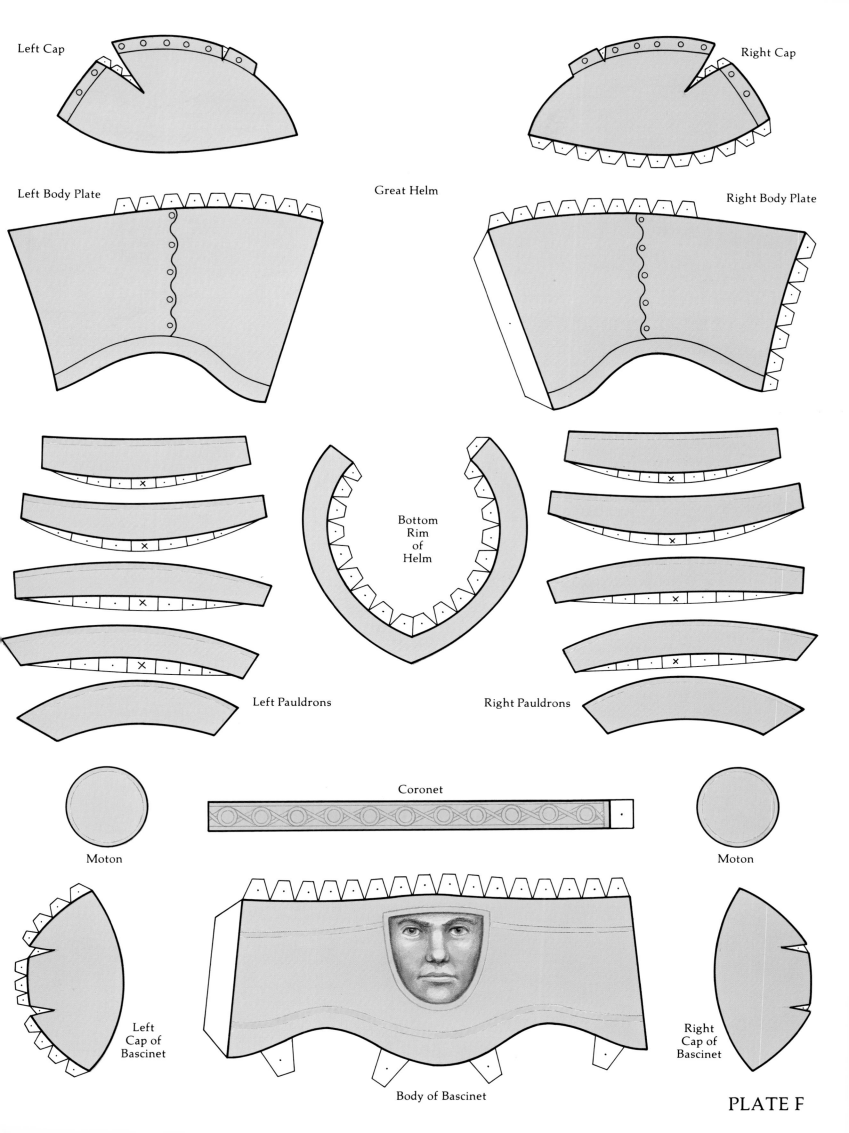

Left Cap

Right Cap

Left Body Plate

Great Helm

Right Body Plate

Bottom
Rim
of
Helm

Left Pauldrons

Right Pauldrons

Moton

Coronet

Moton

Left
Cap of
Bascinet

Right
Cap of
Bascinet

Body of Bascinet

PLATE F

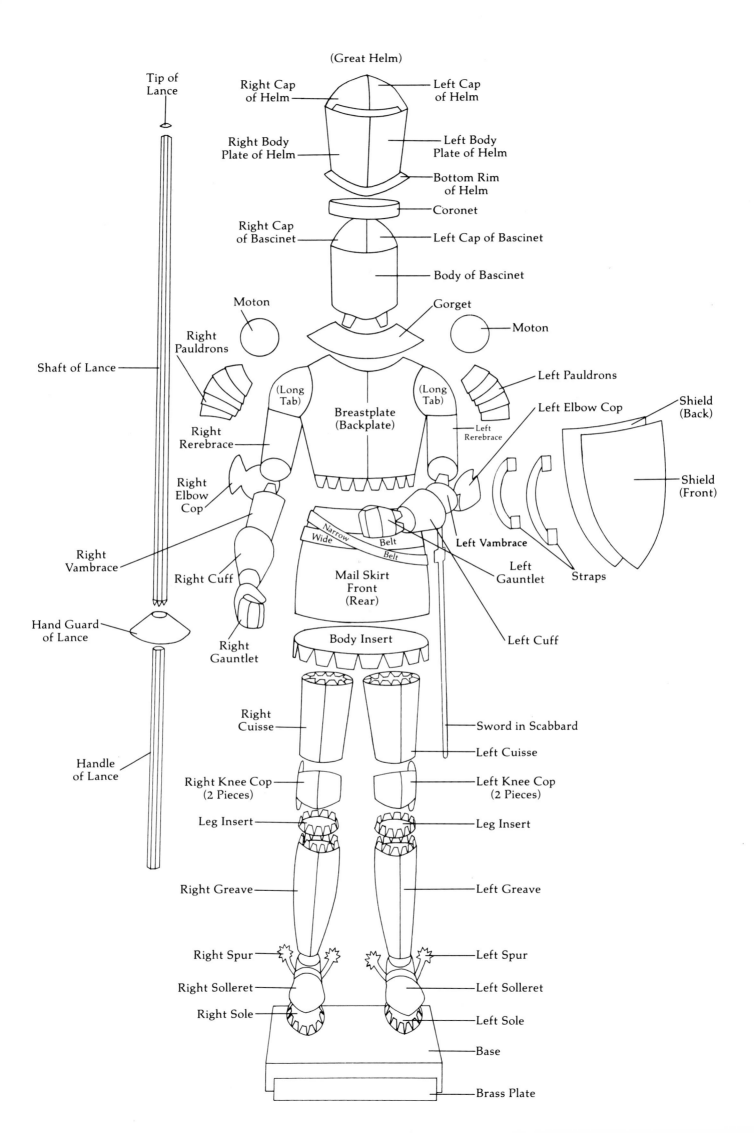

(Great Helm)

Tip of Lance

Right Cap of Helm — Left Cap of Helm

Right Body Plate of Helm — Left Body Plate of Helm

Bottom Rim of Helm

Coronet

Right Cap of Bascinet — Left Cap of Bascinet

Body of Bascinet

Shaft of Lance

Moton — Gorget — Moton

Right Pauldrons — Left Pauldrons

(Long Tab) — Breastplate (Backplate) — (Long Tab)

Left Elbow Cop

Shield (Back)

Right Rerebrace — Left Rerebrace

Right Elbow Cop — Left Vambrace

Shield (Front)

Right Vambrace — Narrow Wide — Belt — Belt

Right Cuff — Mail Skirt Front (Rear) — Left Cuff

Left Gauntlet — Straps

Hand Guard of Lance — Body Insert

Right Gauntlet — Left Cuff

Right Cuisse — Sword in Scabbard

Handle of Lance — Left Cuisse

Right Knee Cop (2 Pieces) — Left Knee Cop (2 Pieces)

Leg Insert — Leg Insert

Right Greave — Left Greave

Right Spur — Left Spur

Right Solleret — Left Solleret

Right Sole — Left Sole

Base

Brass Plate